W9-CPY-759

THE
BEST EVER

KNOCK-KNOCK JOKES

for kids

BOB PHILLIPS

HARVEST HOUSE PUBLISHERS

EUGENE, OREGON

Cover by Dugan Design Group, Bloomington, Minnesota

Cover and interior photo © iStockphoto.com / traveler 1116

Santa

chold I have all the DS game in the worrld. thak you.

THE BEST EVER KNOCK-KNOCK JOKES FOR KIDS

Published by Harvest House Publishers
Eugene, Oregon 97402
www.harvesthousepublishers.com

ISBN 978-0-7369-2772-7

Printed in the United States of America

10 11 12 13 14 15 16 17 18 / BP-NI / 10 9 8 7 6 5 4 3

Contents

Santa I wish
I had a Ds.
Ehold I have
a Ds.

Who's There?

Knock, knock.
Who's there?
Aaron.
Aaron who?
Aaron the barber's floor.

≥ ≤

Knock, knock.
Who's there?
Abyssinia.
Abyssinia who?
Abyssinia around.

≥ ≤

Knock, knock.
Who's there?
Ada.
Ada who?
Ada lot for breakfast.

≥ ≤

Knock, knock.
Who's there?
Adeline.
Adeline who?
Adeline extra to the letter.

⇒ ⇐

Knock, knock.
Who's there?
Aesop.
Aesop who?
Aesop I saw a puddy cat.

⇒ ⇐

Knock, knock.
Who's there?
Aida.
Aida who?
Aida huge breakfast before going to school.

⇒ ⇐

Knock, knock.
Who's there?
Aida.
Aida who?
Aida whole village because I'm a monster.

⇒ ⇐

Knock, knock.
Who's there?
Al.
Al who?
Al lied, and it got me in a lot of trouble

≳ ≲

Knock, knock.
Who's there?
Al.
Al who?
Al be seeing you.

≳ ≲

Knock, knock.
Who's there?
Al.
Al who?
Al go home if you're not nice to me.

≳ ≲

Knock, knock.
Who's there?
Alan.
Alan who?
Alan in a mud puddle and got all dirty.

≳ ≲

Knock, knock.
Who's there?
Alan.
Alan who?
Alan't my lesson not to jump over mud puddles.

Knock, knock.
Who's there?
Alaska.
Alaska who?
Alaska your mother if you can come out and play.

Knock, knock.
Who's there?
Alaska.
Alaska who?
Alaska your mother more than one time if it will
    help!

Knock, knock.
Who's there?
Alaska.
Alaska who?
Alaska your father if your mother is not home.

Stop All the Racket!

Knock, knock.
Who's there?
Baby.
Baby who?
Baby love, my baby love…so much for my singing.

≥ ∈

Knock, knock.
Who's there?
Baby Owl.
Baby Owl who?
Baby Owl see you later, and maybe I won't.

≥ ∈

Knock, knock.
Who's there?
Bach.
Bach who?
Bach to work and earn your allowance.

≥ ∈

Knock, knock.
Who's there?
Bass.
Bass who?
Bass-ball, hot dogs, and apple pie are all-American treats.

≥ ≤

Knock, knock.
Who's there?
Bassoon.
Bassoon who?
Bassoon things will be better.

≥ ≤

Knock, knock.
Who's there?
Bat.
Bat who?
Bat you'll never guess in a million years.

≥ ≤

Knock, knock.
Who's there?
Bayou.
Bayou who?
Did you make up these jokes bayou self?

≥ ≤

Knock, knock.
Who's there?
Bea.
Bea who?
Beacause I'm worth it.

➣ ➤

Knock, knock.
Who's there?
Bea.
Bea who?
Beat your head against a wall.

➣ ➤

Knock, knock.
Who's there?
Bea.
Bea who?
Beatle Bailey was a silly cartoon character.

➣ ➤

Knock, knock.
Who's there?
Beacon.
Beacon who?
Beacon-siderate of me when you open the door.

➣ ➤

Knock, knock.
Who's there?
Bean.
Bean who?
Bean standing out here for a long time.

⋹ ⋵

Knock, knock.
Who's there?
Bean.
Bean who?
Bean working very hard today.

⋹ ⋵

Knock, knock.
Who's there?
Bean.
Bean who?
Bean to any good movies lately?

⋹ ⋵

Knock, knock.
Who's there?
Bean.
Bean who?
Bean fishing lately?

⋹ ⋵

Knock, knock.
Who's there?
Beaver E.
Beaver E who?
Beaver E quiet and nobody will find us.

≥ ∈

Knock, knock.
Who's there?
Becca.
Becca who?
Becca and eggs is what I had for breakfast.

≥ ∈

Knock, knock.
Who's there?
BN.
BN who?
BN at school on time is very important.

≥ ∈

Can Someone Get the Door?

Knock, knock.
Who's there?
Canoe.
Canoe who?
Canoe tell me another knock-knock joke?

Knock, knock.
Who's there?
Canoe.
Canoe who?
Canoe lend me five dollars? I'm broke.

Knock, knock.
Who's there?
Canon.
Canon who?
Canon open the door before I freeze to death out here?

Knock, knock.
Who's there?
Cantaloupe.
Cantaloupe who?
Cantaloupe with you. You don't even know
    my name.

≥ ≤

Knock, knock.
Who's there?
Carlene.
Carlene who?
Carlene against the wall? I'm very tired.

≥ ≤

Knock, knock.
Who's there?
Carlo.
Carlo who?
Carlo-ad of junk is in your front yard.

≥ ≤

Knock, knock.
Who's there?
Carol.
Carol who?
Carol go down the road if you turn the ignition key!

≥ ≤

Knock, knock.
Who's there?
Caroline.
Caroline who?
Caroline of rope with me so I can tie you up.

≳ ≲

Knock, knock.
Who's there?
Carrie.
Carrie who?
Carrie me home, I'm tired.

≳ ≲

Knock, knock.
Who's there?
Carrie.
Carrie who?
Carrie a torch in the Olympic parade.

≳ ≲

Knock, knock.
Who's there?
Carrie.
Carrie who?
Carrie on telling me some of your knock-knock
    jokes.

≳ ≲

Knock, knock.
Who's there?
Carson.
Carson who?
Carsonogenic sounds like poison to me.

Knock, knock.
Who's there?
Cartoon.
Cartoon who?
Cartoon up just fine. It runs like a top now.

Knock, knock.
Who's there?
Cash.
Cash who?
Cash me if you can.

Knock, knock.
Who's there?
Cash.
Cash who?
I knew you were nuts.

Knock, knock.
Who's there?
Cash.
Cash who?
What's the matter? Do you have a cold?

≫ ≪

Knock, knock.
Who's there?
Cass.
Cass who?
Cass more flies with honey than vinegar.

≫ ≪

Knock, knock.
Who's there?
Cassette.
Cassette who?
Cassette your dinner. I'm sorry.

≫ ≪

Please Leave Me Alone!

Knock, knock.
Who's there?
Dan.
Dan who?
Dan Druff is falling out of your hair.

⋺ ⋲

Knock, knock.
Who's there?
Dan.
Dan who?
Dan Druff shampoo is what you need.

⋺ ⋲

Knock, knock.
Who's there?
Dana.
Dana who?
Dana talk with your mouth full.

⋺ ⋲

Knock, knock.
Who's there?
Dancer.
Dancer who?
Dancer is simple—it's me, silly.

≥ ≤

Knock, knock.
Who's there?
Danielle.
Danielle who?
Danielle so loud. I heard you the first time.

≥ ≤

Knock, knock.
Who's there?
Danielle.
Danielle who?
Danielle at me again…just open the door.

≥ ≤

Knock, knock.
Who's there?
Danielle.
Danielle who?
Danielle at me. It's not my fault you're hard of hearing.

≥ ≤

Knock, knock.
Who's there?
Denise.
Denise who?
Denise are above the ankles.

⇌

Knock, knock.
Who's there?
Dennis.
Dennis who?
Does anyone want to play Dennis with me?
    I've got the rackets and ball.

⇌

Knock, knock.
Who's there?
Dennis.
Dennis who?
Dennis says I need to have a tooth out.

⇌

Knock, knock.
Who's there?
Denmark.
Denmark who?
Den marked your fence with spray paint.

⇌

Knock, knock.
Who's there?
Depp.
Depp who?
"Depp inside"—those are the words I want to hear.

≩ ≤

Knock, knock.
Who's there?
Derek.
Derek who?
"Derek of the Hesperus" is a famous poem by
    Longfellow.

≩ ≤

Knock, knock.
Who's there?
Derive.
Derive who?
Derive slowly—the children are playing in the
    street.

≩ ≤

Knock, knock.
Who's there?
Des.
Des who?
Des no bell. Dat's why I'm knocking.

≩ ≤

Get Off My Property!

Knock, knock.
Who's there?
Ears.
Ears who?
Ears looking at you, kid.

⇒ ⇐

Knock, knock.
Who's there?
Ears.
Ears who?
Ears are what you carry on the side of your head.

⇒ ⇐

Knock, knock.
Who's there?
Eel.
Eel who?
Eel be back.

⇒ ⇐

Knock, knock.
Who's there?
Effie.
Effie who?
Effie you don't let me in, I'm going to tell you
　　another knock-knock joke.

≥ ≤

Knock, knock.
Who's there?
Effie.
Effie who?
Effie'd known you were coming, he'd have stayed
　　at home.

≥ ≤

Knock, knock.
Who's there?
Egg!
Egg who?
Eggsactly the point.

≥ ≤

Knock, knock.
Who's there?
Egg!
Egg who?
Egg-citing to meet you.

≥ ≤

Knock, knock.
Who's there?
Egypt.
Egypt who?
Egypt me out of my allowance.

≥ ≤

Knock, knock.
Who's there?
Egypt.
Egypt who?
Egypt a bit off my best china plate and I'm mad
    about it.

≥ ≤

Knock, knock.
Who's there?
Egypt.
Egypt who?
Egypt you when he sold you a broken doorbell.

≥ ≤

Knock, knock.
Who's there?
Eileen.
Eileen who?
Eileen Don your bell and broke it. Sorry.

≥ ≤

Knock, knock.
Who's there?
Eileen.
Eileen who?
Eileen on a cane because I have a sore foot!

⇒ ⇐

Knock, knock.
Who's there?
Eileen.
Eileen who?
Eileen over to tie my shoes.

⇒ ⇐

Knock, knock.
Who's there?
Eisenhower.
Eisenhower who?
Eisenhower late for school this morning. I missed
the bus.

⇒ ⇐

Knock, knock.
Who's there?
Elaine.
Elaine who?
Elaine in the country is where I ride my horse.

⇒ ⇐

I'm Not Home!

Knock, knock.
Who's there?
Felix.
Felix who?
Felix-cited all over.

≽ ≼

Knock, knock.
Who's there?
Felix.
Felix who?
Felix his fingers one more time I'll scream.

≽ ≼

Knock, knock.
Who's there?
Ferdie.
Ferdie who?
Ferdie last time, open this door.

≽ ≼

Knock, knock.
Who's there?
Ferdinand.
Ferdinand who?
Ferdinand beats two in the bush.

≷

Knock, knock.
Who's there?
Fergie.
Fergie who?
Fergie-dness sake let me in. I've been out here for an hour.

≷

Knock, knock.
Who's there?
Ferrer.
Ferrer who?
Ferrer'vrything there is a season.

≷

Knock, knock.
Who's there?
Ferris.
Ferris who?
Ferris fair, you win.

≷

Knock, knock.
Who's there?
Few.
Few who?
Few, what is that awful smell?

≷ ≶

Knock, knock.
Who's there?
Few.
Few who?
Few only knew, you wouldn't keep me outside.

≷ ≶

Knock, knock.
Who's there?
Fez.
Fez who?
Fez me—that's who.

≷ ≶

Knock, knock.
Who's there?
Fiddle.
Fiddle who?
Fiddle make you happy, I'll tell you someday.

≷ ≶

Knock, knock.
Who's there?
Fiddle.
Fiddle who?
Fiddle secrets are hard to keep from other people.

≥ ∈

Knock, knock.
Who's there?
Fiddle.
Fiddle who?
Fiddle-dee-dee.

≥ ∈

Knock, knock.
Who's there?
Fiddlesticks.
Fiddlesticks who?
Fiddlesticks out of the bottom of the bed if you're
    too tall.

≥ ∈

Knock, knock.
Who's there?
Fido.
Fido who?
Fido is the name of my dog.

≥ ∈

Knock, knock.
Who's there?
Fido.
Fido who?
Fido known you were coming I'd have left the
     door open.

⇒ ⇐

Knock, knock.
Who's there?
Fifi.
Fifi who?
Fifi-ling cold. L-l-let me in.

⇒ ⇐

Knock, knock.
Who's there?
Figger.
Figger who?
Figger it out for yourself.

⇒ ⇐

Knock, knock.
Who's there?
Figs.
Figs who?
Figs the doorbell. It's broken.

⇒ ⇐

I Can't Stand the Knocking!

Knock, knock.
Who's there?
Gena.
Gena who?
Genarator is what is needed when the lights go
   out.

≥ ≤

Knock, knock.
Who's there?
Gene.
Gene who?
Genealogy is what you'll need to find out who I
   am.

≥ ≤

Knock, knock.
Who's there?
General.
General who?
General Lee I don't mind hearing another knock-
knock joke.

≥ ≤

Knock, knock.
Who's there?
Genoa.
Genoa who?
Genoa any new jokes?

≥ ≤

Knock, knock.
Who's there?
Geordie.
Geordie who?
Geordie-rectly to jail, do not pass go, do not
collect $200.

≥ ≤

Knock, knock.
Who's there?
George.
George who?
George of the Light Brigade is a great story.

≥ ≤

33

Knock, knock.
Who's there?
Gerald.
Gerald who?
Gerald friend telling another crazy knock-knock
    joke

⇛ ⇚

Knock, knock.
Who's there?
Gerald.
Gerald who?
Gerald washed up telling these jokes.

⇛ ⇚

Knock, knock.
Who's there?
Gertie.
Gertie who?
Gertie laundry needs to be washed.

⇛ ⇚

Knock, knock.
Who's there?
Ghana.
Ghana who?
Ghana go to the soccer game. Do you want to
    come?

⇛ ⇚

Knock, knock.
Who's there?
Ghent.
Ghent who?
Ghent out of here as fast as you can.

≥ ≤

Knock, knock.
Who's there?
Ghost.
Ghost who?
Ghost to coast air travel takes about four to five
    hours.

≥ ≤

Knock, knock.
Who's there?
Ghoul.
Ghoul who?
Ghoulpost is what people kick a soccer ball between.

≥ ≤

Knock, knock.
Who's there?
Ghoul.
Ghoul who?
Ghoulpost saved the ball from going into the net.

≥ ≤

Knock, knock.
Who's there?
Gibbon.
Gibbon who?
Are you gibbon me a hard time?

⋺ ⋹

Knock, knock.
Who's there?
Ginastera.
Ginastera who?
Ginastera at the people!

⋺ ⋹

Knock, knock.
Who's there?
Ginny.
Ginny who?
Ginny-body tell better knock-knock jokes, please?

⋺ ⋹

Knock, knock.
Who's there?
Gino.
Gino who?
Gino me. Now open the door.

⋺ ⋹

If You Keep Knocking, Beware of the Dog!

Knock, knock.
Who's there?
Haifa.
Haifa who?
Haifa piece of cake is better than none.

≥ ≤

Knock, knock.
Who's there?
Hair.
Hair who?
Hair today—gone tomorrow. That's what the bald
    man says.

≥ ≤

Knock, knock.
Who's there?
Hairdo.
Hairdo who?
Hairdo some weird stuff. Can I borrow your brush?

⇒ ⇐

Knock, knock.
Who's there?
Hiram.
Hiram who?
Hiram tired of all these jokes.

⇒ ⇐

Knock, knock.
Who's there?
Haiti.
Haiti who?
Haiti see you laugh so hard at all these jokes.

⇒ ⇐

Knock, knock.
Who's there?
Hal.
Hal who?
Hal about opening the door?

⇒ ⇐

Knock, knock.
Who's there?
Halifax.
Halifax who?
Halifax you if you fax me.

≥ ∈

Knock, knock.
Who's there?
Hallie.
Hallie who?
Hallie-tosis—your breath stinks!

≥ ∈

Knock, knock.
Who's there?
Hammond.
Hammond who?
Hammond cheese on toast, please.

≥ ∈

Knock, knock.
Who's there?
Hand.
Hand who?
Hand over your money. This is a stick-up.

≥ ∈

Knock, knock.
Who's there?
Handel.
Handel who?
Handel me with care. I'm very fragile.

⇉ ⇇

Knock, knock.
Who's there?
Handi.
Handi who?
Handiman needs to fix your doorbell.

⇉ ⇇

Knock, knock.
Who's there?
Handsome.
Handsome who?
Handsome chips through the keyhole. I'm hungry.

⇉ ⇇

Knock, knock.
Who's there?
Hank.
Hank who?
Hank misbehavin' myself out here.

⇉ ⇇

Knock, knock.
Who's there?
Hank.
Hank who?
Hanker's away is what the sailor says.

⇒ ⇐

Knock, knock.
Who's there?
Hannah.
Hannah who?
Hannah me something to drink. I'm thirsty.

⇒ ⇐

Knock, knock.
Who's there?
Hannah.
Hannah who?
Hannah—the one who lives in Montana.

⇒ ⇐

Knock, knock.
Who's there?
Hannah.
Hannah who?
Hannah me a piece of candy please.

⇒ ⇐

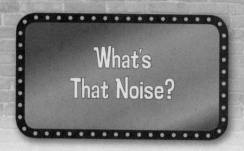

What's That Noise?

Knock, knock.
Who's there?
Ina.
Ina who?
Ina minute, I'm going to knock this door down.

≥ ≤

Knock, knock.
Who's there?
Ina.
Ina who?
Ina 'nother minute, I'm going to scream.

≥ ≤

Knock, knock.
Who's there?
India.
India who?
India night time, I go to sleep. What do you do?

≥ ≤

Knock, knock.
Who's there?
India!
India who?
India good old summertime!

⇒ ∈

Knock, knock.
Who's there?
Indiana.
Indiana who?
Indiana'ls of history, you'll be remembered for
being so weird.

⇒ ∈

Knock, knock.
Who's there?
Indonesia.
Indonesia who?
I look at you and get week Indonesia.

⇒ ∈

Knock, knock.
Who's there?
Ines.
Ines who?
Ines-special place, your parents hide your
Christmas presents.

⇒ ∈

Knock, knock.
Who's there?
Ingrid.
Ingrid who?
Ingrid sorrow I have to leave you.

⋙ ⋘

Knock, knock.
Who's there?
Innuendo.
Innuendo who?
If you don't open the door, I'll climb innuendo.

⋙ ⋘

Knock, knock.
Who's there?
Insect.
Insect who?
Insect is on your collar, and it's about to climb up
your neck.

⋙ ⋘

Knock, knock.
Who's there?
Into.
Into who?
Into minutes you're going to get into trouble if
you don't let me in.

⋙ ⋘

Knock, knock.
Who's there?
Iona.
Iona who?
Iona great train set.

⋝ ⋜

Knock, knock.
Who's there?
Iona.
Iona who?
Iona police dog, and he's going to bite you if you
    don't let me in.

⋝ ⋜

Knock, knock.
Who's there?
Iowa.
Iowa who?
Iowa you a dollar, and you won't get it if you keep
    the door locked.

⋝ ⋜

I'm Not Letting You In!

Knock, knock.
Who's there?
Jeannette.
Jeannette who?
Jeannette has too many holes, all the fish will
    swim out.

⋰ ⋱

Knock, knock.
Who's there?
Jeer.
Jeer who?
Jeer about the chicken that crossed the road?
    He wanted to get to the other side.

⋰ ⋱

Knock, knock.
Who's there?
Jeffrey.
Jeffrey who?
Jeffrey time I knock, you ask the same question.

≷

Knock, knock.
Who's there?
Jelly Bean.
Jelly Bean who?
Jelly Bean to the zoo lately?

≷

Knock, knock.
Who's there?
Jenelle.
Jenelle who?
Jenelle the picture of Spider-Man on the wall?

≷

Knock, knock.
Who's there?
Jenny.
Jenny who?
Jenny'd any help opening the door?

≷

Knock, knock.
Who's there?
Jenny.
Jenny who?
Jennymen always open the door for ladies.

≳ ≲

Knock, knock.
Who's there?
Jenny Lind!
Jenny Lind who?
Jenny, Lind me some money I'm broke.

≳ ≲

Knock, knock.
Who's there?
Jerky.
Jerky who?
Jerky the door open so I can come in.

≳ ≲

Knock, knock.
Who's there?
Jerky.
Jerky who?
Jerky may work in the lock, but mine doesn't.

≳ ≲

Knock, knock.
Who's there?
Jerome.
Jerome who?
Jerome around your house and open the door.

≥ ≤

Knock, knock.
Who's there?
Jerrold.
Jerrold who?
Jerrold friend…you remember me, don't you?

≥ ≤

Knock, knock.
Who's there?
Jerry.
Jerry who?
Jerry funny knock-knock joke, don't you think?

≥ ≤

Knock, knock.
Who's there?
Jerry.
Jerry who?
Jerry me into the house. I tired of standing out
here.

≥ ≤

Knock, knock.
Who's there?
Jess.
Jess who?
Jess me and my shadow—that's who.

≥ ≤

Knock, knock.
Who's there?
Jess.
Jess who?
I give up. Who?

≥ ≤

Knock, knock.
Who's there?
Jess.
Jess who?
Jessebell. Remember, she was a wicked queen from the Bible.

≥ ≤

Knock, knock.
Who's there?
Jess.
Jess who?
Jess one of your good friends.

≥ ≤

All This Knocking Is Getting Old!

Knock, knock.
Who's there?
Ken.
Ken who?
Ken I come in, or do I have to climb through a
    window?

⇒ ⇐

Knock, knock.
Who's there?
Kendall.
Kendall who?
Kendall and Barbie doll go together.

⇒ ⇐

Knock, knock.
Who's there?
Kennedy.
Kennedy who?
Kennedy crazy jokes ever be stopped?

≥ ∈

Knock, knock.
Who's there?
Kenneth.
Kenneth who?
Kenneth you come out and play?

≥ ∈

Knock, knock.
Who's there?
Kenny.
Kenny who?
Kenny body home in there?

≥ ∈

Knock, knock.
Who's there?
Kent.
Kent who?
Kent you tell who it is?

≥ ∈

Knock, knock.
Who's there?
Kentucky.
Kentucky who?
Kentucky come out to play ball?

⋺⋹

Knock, knock.
Who's there?
Kentucky.
Kentucky who?
Kentucky too well. I have a sore throat.

⋺⋹

Knock, knock.
Who's there?
Kenya.
Kenya who?
Kenya loan me your skateboard?

⋺⋹

Knock, knock.
Who's there?
Kenya.
Kenya who?
Kenya come up with your own knock-knock joke?

⋺⋹

Knock, knock.
Who's there?
Kermit.
Kermit who?
Kermit a crime, and you'll get locked up by the
     police.

＞ ＜

Knock, knock.
Who's there?
Kerri.
Kerri who?
Will you Kerri my backpack for me?

＞ ＜

Knock, knock.
Who's there?
Kerry.
Kerry who?
Kerry me up the stairs, will you? I have a tummy
     ache.

＞ ＜

Knock, knock.
Who's there?
Ketchup.
Ketchup who?
Ketchup with me and I'll tell you.

＞ ＜

Knock, knock.
Who's there?
Ketchup.
Ketchup who?
Ketchup the tree again…better get a ladder to get
  her down.

⇒ ⇐

Knock, knock.
Who's there?
Kevin.
Kevin who?
Kevin got any idea who it is, do you?

⇒ ⇐

Knock, knock.
Who's there?
Keyboard.
Keyboard who?
Keyboard on my computer won't work.

⇒ ⇐

Knock, knock.
Who's there?
Khan.
Khan who?
Khan you stop with all these knock-knock jokes?

⇒ ⇐

Stop That Banging!

Knock, knock.
Who's there?
Lee King.
Lee King who?
Lee King chocolate off the cake spoon is lots of fun.

≥ ≤

Knock, knock.
Who's there?
Lego.
Lego who?
Lego of me, and I'll tell you.

≥ ≤

Knock, knock.
Who's there?
Leif.
Leif who?
Leif me alone with all these questions.

≥ ≤

Knock, knock.
Who's there?
Les.
Les who?
Les me call you sweetheart!

⇉ ⇇

Knock, knock.
Who's there?
Les.
Les who?
The Les knock-knock jokes, the better.

⇉ ⇇

Knock, knock.
Who's there?
Les.
Les who?
Les go for a swim.

⇉ ⇇

Knock, knock.
Who's there?
Leslie.
Leslie who?
Leslie town and go ride a horse.

⇉ ⇇

Knock It Off!

Knock, knock.
Who's there?
Maine.
Maine who?
Maine I come in now, please?

≥ ≤

Knock, knock.
Who's there?
Major.
Major who?
Major answer, didn't I?

≥ ≤

Knock, knock.
Who's there?
Major.
Major who?
Majority rules over the minority.

≥ ≤

Knock, knock.
Who's there?
Mako.
Mako who?
Mako your dog stop barking.

><

Knock, knock.
Who's there?
Malcolm.
Malcolm who?
Malcome you didn't do your homework?

><

Knock, knock.
Who's there?
Mali.
Mali who?
Mali down because she was tired after washing the
    dishes.

><

Knock, knock.
Who's there?
Malt.
Malt who?
Malt-esers the girls and makes them mad.

><

Knock, knock.
Who's there?
Mamie.
Mamie who?
Mamie I'll tell you, and maybe I won't.

⋑ ⋐

Knock, knock.
Who's there?
Man.
Man who?
Man, why are you locking me out?

⋑ ⋐

Knock, knock.
Who's there?
Manchu.
Manchu who?
Manchu your food with your mouth closed.

⋑ ⋐

Knock, knock.
Who's there?
Mandy.
Mandy who?
Mandy lifeboats! We're sinking fast!

⋑ ⋐

Knock, knock.
Who's there?
Manitoba.
Manitoba who?
Manitoba me a very funny knock-knock joke.

⇉ ⇇

Knock, knock.
Who's there?
Manny.
Manny who?
Manny people keep asking me that same question.

⇉ ⇇

Knock, knock.
Who's there?
Manny.
Manny who?
Manny are called, but few are chosen.

⇉ ⇇

Knock, knock.
Who's there?
Manuel.
Manuel who?
Manuel be sorry if you don't open this door!

⇉ ⇇

The Door Is Shut!

Knock, knock.
Who's there?
Nate.
Nate who?
Nature boy that's who.

≥ ≤

Knock, knock.
Who's there?
NE.
NE who?
NE body but me.

≥ ≤

Knock, knock.
Who's there?
Neal.
Neal who?
Nealing and praying are a good idea.

≥ ≤

Knock, knock.
Who's there?
Nebraska.
Nebraska who?
Nebraska girl for a date. She might say yes.

≥ ≤

Knock, knock.
Who's there?
Ned.
Ned who?
The horses ran Ned and neck.

≥ ≤

Knock, knock.
Who's there?
Nell.
Nell who?
Nell is something you pound into a board, silly.

≥ ≤

Knock, knock.
Who's there?
Nestle.
Nestle who?
Nestle into the soft chair and relax.

≥ ≤

Knock, knock.
Who's there?
Nettie.
Nettie who?
Nettie is what they hit a tennis ball over.

≽ ≼

Knock, knock.
Who's there?
Nettie.
Nettie who?
You're Nettie as a fruitcake.

≽ ≼

Knock, knock.
Who's there?
Nevada.
Nevada who?
Nevada saw you look so bad, you should be in bed.

≽ ≼

Knock, knock.
Who's there?
Newt.
Newt who?
Newton's law of gravity.

≽ ≼

Knock, knock.
Who's there?
Newt.
Newt who?
I like Fig Newtons.

⇒ ⇐

Knock, knock.
Who's there?
Nicholas.
Nicholas who?
Don't you know? Nicholas, the saint that comes at
    Christmas.

⇒ ⇐

Knock, knock.
Who's there?
Nick.
Nick who?
Nick my face while trying to shave.

⇒ ⇐

Knock, knock.
Who's there?
Nick.
Nick who?
Nickle and dime you to death.

⇒ ⇐

Knock, knock.
Who's there?
Nicky.
Nicky who?
My mother collects Nicky nacks.

≥ ≤

Knock, knock.
Who's there?
Noah.
Noah who?
Do you Noah any more knock-knock jokes?

≥ ≤

Knock, knock.
Who's there?
Noah.
Noah who?
If you Noah more jokes…please tell me Noah
    more of them.

≥ ≤

I'm Busy!

Knock, knock.
Who's there?
Ohio.
Ohio who?
"Ohio Silver…away!" That's what the Lone Ranger
    said to his horse.

≥ ≤

Knock, knock.
Who's there?
Okra.
Okra who?
Okra Winfrey.

≥ ≤

Knock, knock.
Who's there?
Olaf.
Olaf who?
Olaf if you think it's that funny!

≥ ≤

Knock, knock.
Who's there?
Olaf!
Olaf who?
Olaf at you when I see your face.

≥ ≤

Knock, knock.
Who's there?
Oldest son.
Oldest son who?
Oldest son shines bright on my old Kentucky
home.

≥ ≤

Knock, knock.
Who's there?
Old King Cole.
Old King Cole who?
Old King Cole, so turn the heat up.

≥ ≤

Knock, knock.
Who's there?
Ole.
Ole who?
"Ole Little Town of Bethlehem."

≥ ≤

Knock, knock.
Who's there?
Olga.
Olga who?
Olga home if you don't open up.

≥ ≤

Knock, knock.
Who's there?
Olga.
Olga who?
Olga way when I'm good and ready.

≥ ≤

Knock, knock.
Who's there?
Olive.
Olive who?
Olive none of your lip.

≥ ≤

Knock, knock.
Who's there?
Olive.
Olive who?
Olive just around the corner.

⇒ ⇐

Knock, knock.
Who's there?
Olive.
Olive who?
Olive in a house where the doorbell works.

⇒ ⇐

Knock, knock.
Who's there?
Olive.
Olive who?
Olive you too, honeybunch.

⇒ ⇐

Knock, knock.
Who's there?
Olive.
Olive who?
Olive a fun life of telling knock-knock jokes.

⇒ ⇐

Knock, knock.
Who's there?
Oliver.
Oliver who?
I'm so sad. Oliver, but she doesn't love me.

⋝ ⋜

Knock, knock.
Who's there?
Oliver.
Oliver who?
Oliver clothes are getting wet. It's pouring out
    here.

⋝ ⋜

Knock, knock.
Who's there?
Oliver.
Oliver who?
Oliver troubles are over. It finally stopped raining.

⋝ ⋜

Knock, knock.
Who's there?
Olivia.
Olivia who?
Olivia me alone.

⋝ ⋜

I'm Not Opening the Door!

Knock, knock.
Who's there?
Parish.
Parish who?
Parish the thought of another knock-knock joke.

⋟ ⋞

Knock, knock.
Who's there?
Parrot.
Parrot who?
Parrots on the ground if you don't pick it up.

⋟ ⋞

Knock, knock.
Who's there?
Parsley.
Parsley who?
Parsley the catsup, please.

⋟ ⋞

Knock, knock.
Who's there?
Parton.
Parton who?
Parton me for telling another knock-knock joke.

≥ ∈

Knock, knock.
Who's there?
Passion.
Passion who?
Passion cars on a busy street can be dangerous.

≥ ∈

Knock, knock.
Who's there?
Passion.
Passion who?
Just passion by and thought I'd pop in.

≥ ∈

Knock, knock.
Who's there?
Passion.
Passion who?
I'm passion out if I hear any more knock-knock jokes.

≥ ∈

Knock, knock.
Who's there?
Pasta.
Pasta who?
Pasta salt, please.

≫ ≪

Knock, knock.
Who's there?
Pastille.
Pastille who?
Pastille next street, and you'll find a pizza parlor.

≫ ≪

Knock, knock.
Who's there?
Pasture.
Pasture who?
Pasture bedtime, isn't it?

≫ ≪

Knock, knock.
Who's there?
Pat.
Pat who?
Pat up your troubles in your old kit bag.

≫ ≪

Knock, knock.
Who's there?
Pat.
Pat who?
Pat'ch up my coat sleeve. It has a hole in it.

≥ ∈

Knock, knock.
Who's there?
Pat.
Pat who?
Pat yourself too hard on the back, and you might
    break your arm.

≥ ∈

Knock, knock.
Who's there?
Pat.
Pat who?
Pat'ie cake is a game that babies play.

≥ ∈

Knock, knock.
Who's there?
Patrick.
Patrick who?
Patricked me into telling another knock-knock
    joke.

≥ ∈

That Door Is Expensive!

Knock, knock.
Who's there?
R-2.
R-2 who?
R-2 is a character in Star Wars.

⇌

Knock, knock.
Who's there?
Rabbit.
Rabbit who?
Rabbit up carefully—it's a present.

⇌

Knock, knock.
Who's there?
Radio.
Radio who?
Radio not, here I come!

⇌

Knock, knock.
Who's there?
Rain.
Rain who?
Rain dear—as in Rudolph the red-nosed rain dear.

∋ ∈

Knock, knock.
Who's there?
Raleigh.
Raleigh who?
Raleigh round the flag boys.

∋ ∈

Knock, knock.
Who's there?
Red.
Red who?
Reddy, aim, fire.

∋ ∈

Knock, knock.
Who's there?
Red.
Red who?
Red peppers. Isn't that a hot one?

∋ ∈

Knock, knock.
Who's there?
Reed.
Reed who?
Reed between the lines, and you'll find the answer.

∋ ∈

Knock, knock.
Who's there?
Reed.
Reed who?
Reedturn to sender. Address unknown.

∋ ∈

Knock, knock.
Who's there?
Rena.
Rena who?
Rena this bell doesn't do any good…nobody
    answers the door.

∋ ∈

Knock, knock.
Who's there?
Renato.
Renato who?
Renato milk. Could I borrow some?

∋ ∈

Knock, knock.
Who's there?
Renato.
Renato who?
Renato gas last night, and I had to walk a mile.

Knock, knock.
Who's there?
Rene.
Rene who?
Rene the marathon and won a prize

Knock, knock.
Who's there?
Reuben.
Reuben who?
Reuben my eyes because I'm tired.

Knock, knock.
Who's there?
Rhoda.
Rhoda who?
Rhoda boat as fast as you can.

I'm Coming
– Just Kidding!

Knock, knock.
Who's there?
S.
S who?
SOS. I need help to get into your house.

⇒ ⇐

Knock, knock.
Who's there?
Sally.
Sally who?
Sally question you keep asking.

⇒ ⇐

Knock, knock.
Who's there?
Salome.
Salome who?
Salome and cheese make great sandwiches.

⇒ ⇐

Knock, knock.
Who's there?
Sam.
Sam who?
Sam person who knocked on the door last time.

≥ ≤

Knock, knock.
Who's there?
Sam.
Sam who?
Sam Francisco, here I come.

≥ ≤

Knock, knock.
Who's there?
Sam.
Sam who?
I left my heart in Sam Francisco.

≥ ≤

Knock, knock.
Who's there?
Sam.
Sam who?
Sam day you'll recognize me.

≥ ≤

Knock, knock.
Who's there?
Sam and Janet.
Sam and Janet who?
Sam and Janet evening, you will meet a stranger.

⋟ ⋞

Knock, knock.
Who's there?
Samson.
Samson who?
Samson you turned out to be.

⋟ ⋞

Knock, knock.
Who's there?
Samuel.
Samuel who?
Samuel be famous for telling knock-knock jokes.

⋟ ⋞

Knock, knock.
Who's there?
Sandra.
Sandra who?
Sandra-bout your toes at the beach.

⋟ ⋞

Knock, knock.
Who's there?
Sandy.
Sandy who?
Sandy locksmith to get this door open.

⇒ ⇐

Knock, knock.
Who's there?
Sandy.
Sandy who?
Sandy door, I just got a splinter.

⇒ ⇐

Knock, knock.
Who's there?
Santa.
Santa who?
Santa email but you never replied.

⇒ ⇐

Can You Afford to Replace My Door?

Knock, knock.
Who's there?
Teachers.
Teachers who?
Teachers for the red, white, and blue. Hip, hip...
    hooray!

⇒ ⇐

Knock, knock.
Who's there?
Teddy.
Teddy who?
Teddy is the beginning of the rest of your life.

⇒ ⇐

Knock, knock.
Who's there?
Teddy.
Teddy who?
Teddy is the name of a bear that I used to have.

⇒ ⇐

Knock, knock.
Who's there?
Teheran.
Teheran who?
Teheran and look me in the eye!

⇒ ⇐

Knock, knock.
Who's there?
Telly.
Telly who?
Telly your friend to come out and play.

⇒ ⇐

Knock, knock.
Who's there?
Ten.
Ten who?
Ten to your own business.

⇒ ⇐

Knock, knock.
Who's there?
Tennessee.
Tennessee who?
Tennessee you tonight?

≥ ≤

Knock, knock.
Who's there?
Tennessee.
Tennessee who?
Tennessee is played at Wimbledon.

≥ ≤

Knock, knock.
Who's there?
Tennis.
Tennis who?
Tennis five plus five.

≥ ≤

Knock, knock.
Who's there?
Teresa.
Teresa who?
Teresa green, and so is grass.

≥ ≤

Knock, knock.
Who's there?
Termite.
Termite who?
Termite be something wrong with your glasses.
It's me!

⇒ ∈

Knock, knock.
Who's there?
Termite.
Termite who?
Termite be more funny knock-knock jokes.

⇒ ∈

Knock, knock.
Who's there?
Terry.
Terry who?
Terry's nothing like a nice big ice-cream cone.

⇒ ∈

Knock, knock.
Who's there?
Tex.
Tex who?
Texedo Junction!

⇒ ∈

Knock, knock.
Who's there?
Tex.
Tex who?
Tex two to tango, you know.

>< ><

Knock, knock.
Who's there?
Texas.
Texas who?
Texas are getting higher every year.

>< ><

Knock, knock.
Who's there?
Thad.
Thad who?
Thad's the way—uh-huh, uh-huh—I like it.

>< ><

Knock, knock.
Who's there?
Thaddeus.
Thaddeus who?
To be or not to be—Thaddeus the question.

>< ><

Knock, knock.
Who's there?
Thais.
Thais who?
Thais an silly question to ask.

➣ ➣

Knock, knock.
Who's there?
Thatcher.
Thatcher who?
Thatcher could get away with another joke, didn't
    you?

➣ ➣

Knock, knock.
Who's there?
Thea.
Thea who?
Thea later, alligator.

➣ ➣

Knock, knock.
Who's there?
Thelonius.
Thelonius who?
Thelonius kid in town because you won't answer
    the door.

➣ ➣

Knock, knock.
Who's there?
Utah.
Utah who?
Utah me when you looked out the window.

>< <

Knock, knock.
Who's there?
Utah.
Utah who?
Utah the board in two, and I'll hammer with
the nail.

>< <

Knock, knock.
Who's there?
Utah.
Utah who?
Utah'aut me how to use a skateboard.

≥ ≤

Knock, knock.
Who's there?
Utah.
Utah who?
Utah'ller than me, but we are about the same
    weight.

≥ ≤

Knock, knock.
Who's there?
Utica.
Utica who?
Utica the high road, and I'll take the low road.

≥ ≤

Knock, knock.
Who's there?
Uva.
Uva who?
Uva bicycle I could borrow?

≥ ≤

Have Some Patience!

Knock, knock.
Who's there?
Veal chop.
Veal chop who?
Veal chop around and see what bargains vee can
   pick up.

≥ ≤

Knock, knock.
Who's there?
Veal chop.
Veal chop who?
Veal chop for some new clothes.

≥ ≤

Knock, knock.
Who's there?
Velvet.
Velvet who?
Velvet, how's my dog doing? Is he sick?

⇒ ⇐

Knock, knock.
Who's there?
Venda.
Venda who?
Venda red, red robin comes bob, bob, bobbing
    along.

⇒ ⇐

Knock, knock.
Who's there?
Venice.
Venice who?
Venice your mother coming home?

⇒ ⇐

Knock, knock.
Who's there?
Vent.
Vent who?
I vent to school this morning. Vhat did you do?

⇒ ⇐

Knock, knock.
Who's there?
Venus.
Venus who?
Venus you ever going to stop telling knock-knock
    jokes?

≥ ≤

Knock, knock.
Who's there?
Vera.
Vera who?
Vera all the flowers gone?

≥ ≤

Knock, knock.
Who's there?
Verdi.
Verdi who?
Verdi been all day?

≥ ≤

Knock, knock.
Who's there?
Vic.
Vic who?
Vic a card—any card, and I'll show you a magic
    trick.

≥ ≤

Knock, knock.
Who's there?
Vicious.
Vicious who?
I vicious you a Merry Christmas.

≥ ∈

Knock, knock.
Who's there?
Victor.
Victor who?
Victor his jeans when he fell off his skateboard.

≥ ∈

Knock, knock.
Who's there?
Victor.
Victor who?
Victor'y is for the winner of the soccer game.

≥ ∈

Knock, knock.
Who's there?
Vidal.
Vidal who?
Vidal like to have you stop with all of these jokes.

≥ ∈

Knock, knock.
Who's there?
Vigor.
Vigor who?
He's much vigor than I thought he'd be.

≥ ≤

Knock, knock.
Who's there?
Vincent.
Vincent who?
Vincent me here to see if I could get in.

≥ ≤

Knock, knock.
Who's there?
Vincent.
Vincent who?
Vincent a key but I lost it on the way over here.

≥ ≤

Knock, knock.
Who's there?
Viola.
Viola who?
Viola sudden, don't you know me?

≥ ≤

The More You Knock, the Less I Want to Answer!

Knock, knock.
Who's there?
Wallace.
Wallace who?
Wallace have ears and can hear all of your secrets.

⇒ ⇐

Knock, knock.
Who's there?
Wallace.
Wallace who?
Wallace saying unkind things about you.

⇒ ⇐

Knock, knock.
Who's there?
Walnut.
Walnut who?
Walnut too strong, don't lean on it.

≥ ≤

Knock, knock.
Who's there?
Walnuts.
Walnuts who?
We're walnuts around here.

≥ ≤

Knock, knock.
Who's there?
Walt.
Walt who?
"Walting Matilda" is a silly song.

≥ ≤

Knock, knock.
Who's there?
Walt.
Walt who?
Walt till your father gets home…boy, you're in
    trouble.

≥ ≤

Knock, knock.
Who's there?
Walter.
Walter who?
Walterdash is a silly saying.

⇉ ⇇

Knock, knock.
Who's there?
Walter.
Walter who?
There's Walter-wall carpeting in our house.

⇉ ⇇

Knock, knock.
Who's there?
Wanda.
Wanda who?
Wanda off, and you'll get lost.

⇉ ⇇

Knock, knock.
Who's there?
Wanda.
Wanda who?
Wanda go for a walk with me?

⇉ ⇇

Knock, knock.
Who's there?
Wanda.
Wanda who?
Wanda buy a cheap bike? It's got no wheels.

⇒ ⇐

Knock, knock.
Who's there?
Wanda.
Wanda who?
Wanda around while I climb through the window.

⇒ ⇐

Knock, knock.
Who's there?
Wanda.
Wanda who?
Wanda buy some Girl Scout cookies?

⇒ ⇐

Knock, knock.
Who's there?
Wannetta.
Wannetta who?
Wannetta time, please.

⇒ ⇐

Knock, knock.
Who's there?
Ward.
Ward who?
Ward do you want?

≳ ≲

Knock, knock.
Who's there?
Ward.
Ward who?
Ward'robe is where I keep all of my clothes.

≳ ≲

Knock, knock.
Who's there?
Warner.
Warner who?
Warner a lift to the mall? My car's outside.

≳ ≲

Knock, knock.
Who's there?
Warner.
Warner who?
Warner you coming out to play?

≳ ≲

Isn't Your Hand Getting Tired?

Knock, knock.
Who's there?
Yma.
Yma who?
Yma Sumac for wrecking her car.

≥ ≤

Knock, knock.
Who's there?
Yoda.
Yoda who?
Yoda le lee whoo.

≥ ≤

Knock, knock.
Who's there?
Yoda.
Yoda who?
Yoda is a character from Star Wars. Don't you
    remember?

⇒ ∈

Knock, knock.
Who's there?
Yogi Bear.
Yogi Bear who?
Yogi Bear, and he's getting very cold.

⇒ ∈

Knock, knock.
Who's there?
Yoke.
Yoke who?
The yoke's on you! Ha, ha, ha.

⇒ ∈

Knock, knock.
Who's there?
Yolanda.
Yolanda who?
Yolanda me some money, and I can't pay you back.
    Sorry.

⇒ ∈

Knock, knock.
Who's there?
Yolanda.
Yolanda who?
Yolanda on your back when you step on a banana.

⋺ ⋲

Knock, knock.
Who's there?
Yolande.
Yolande who?
Yolande me a dollar. I'll pay you back next week.

⋺ ⋲

Knock, knock.
Who's there?
York.
York who?
York going to open the door, aren't you?

⋺ ⋲

Knock, knock.
Who's there?
You.
You who?
You who! Is there anybody in?

⋺ ⋲

Knock, knock.
Who's there?
You.
You who?
Who's that calling out? You don't have to yell
    about it.

≥ ≤

Knock, knock.
Who's there?
You.
You who?
Are you calling me?

≥ ≤

Knock, knock.
Who's there?
You.
You who?
You who to you too.

≥ ≤

Knock, knock.
Who's there?
You!
You who?
Did you call?

≥ ≤

Knock, knock.
Who's there?
Your pencil.
Your pencil who?
Your pencil fall down if you don't wear a belt or
    suspenders.

⇒ ⇐

Knock, knock.
Who's there?
Yucatan.
Yucatan who?
Yucatan very fast and even get sunburned without
    suntan lotion.

⇒ ⇐

Knock, knock.
Who's there?
Yucatan.
Yucatan who?
Yucatan fool some people all of the time.

⇒ ⇐

Knock, knock.
Who's there?
Yucca.
Yucca who?
Yucca catch more flies with honey than vinegar.

⇒ ⇐

Too Many Knock-Knock Jokes!

Knock, knock.
Who's there?
Zizi.
Zizi who?
Zizi to know when you open the door.

⇒ ⇐

Knock, knock.
Who's there?
Zoe.
Zoe who?
Zoe doesn't recognize my voice by now?

⇒ ⇐

Knock, knock.
Who's there?
Zoe.
Zoe who?
Zoe a button on your shirt.

⇉ ⇇

Knock, knock.
Who's there?
Zoe.
Zoe who?
Zoe by now you should know who it is.

⇉ ⇇

Knock, knock.
Who's there?
Zombie.
Zombie who?
Zombies make honey, others are queens!

⇉ ⇇

Knock, knock.
Who's there?
Zone.
Zone who?
His zone shadow scares him.

⇉ ⇇

Knock, knock.
Who's there?
Zookeeper.
Zookeeper who?
Zookeeper away from me.

⋺ ⋹

Knock, knock.
Who's there?
Zoom.
Zoom who?
Zoom did you expect?

⋺ ⋹

Knock, knock.
Who's there?
Zsa Zsa.
Zsa Zsa who?
Zsa Zsa last knock-knock joke—well, not really.

⋺ ⋹

Knock, knock.
Who's there?
Zubin.
Zubin who?
Zubin eating garlic again?

⋺ ⋹

Other Books by Bob Phillips

For more information, send a self-addressed
stamped envelope to

Family Services
P.O. Box 9363
Fresno, California 93702